Mark J. Rauzon

Parrots Around the World

Franklin Watts - A Division of Grolier Publishing
New York • London • Hong Kong • Sydney • Danbury, Connecticut

For Maya

Photographs ©: Brian Kenney: 6, 7, 13, 15; Kevin Schafer: 5 top left, 5 bottom right, 5 bottom left; Lynn M. Stone: 27; Mark J. Rauzon: 17, 19, 37; Peter Arnold Inc.: 39 (Gerard Lacz), 43 (Kevin Schafer), 42 (Roland Seitre); Photo Researchers: 29 (John S. Dunning), cover (Labat J. M. Jacana), 23 (Joyce Photographics), 5 top right (G. C. Kelley), 20, 21 (Tom McHugh), 33 (Anthony Mercieca), 41 (E. Hanumantha Rao); Tony Stone Images: 25 (Daniel J. Cox), 1 (Art Wolfe); Visuals Unlimited: 35 (Gary Meszaros) 31.

Illustrations by Jose Gonzales and Steve Savage

The photo on the cover shows a brightly colored parrot perching on a branch. The photo on the title page shows male and female eclectus parrots on a branch.

Visit Franklin Watts on the Internet at:
http://publishing.grolier.com

Library of Congress Cataloging-in-Publication Data

Rauzon, Mark J.
    Parrots around the world / Mark J. Rauzon
       p. cm. — (Animals in order)
    Includes bibliographical references and index.
    Summary: An introduction to parrots, a taxonomic order of birds, that includes descriptions of fifteen species and recommendations for finding, identifying, and observing them.
    ISBN 0-531-11688-3 (lib. bdg.)   0-531-13958-1 (pbk.)
1. Parrots—Juvenile literature. [1. Parrots.] I. Title. II. Series.
QL696.P7 R374   2001
598.7'1—dc21   99-05725

Contents

What Is a Parrot?

Imagine that you are walking through the Amazon rain forest of South America. Loud screams from high in the treetops attract your attention. Suddenly, two big, beautiful macaws fly into sight. Their wings flash brilliant red in the sunlight. From a hole in a dead tree, two red-fronted parakeets peer out to see what is causing the commotion. Above them, a toucan hops along a tree branch. Its beak is as big as a banana. Overhead, a flock of tiny parrotlets race by. The little birds screech loudly as they fly.

Those tropical birds are all colorful, but they are not all parrots. Look at the four birds shown on the next page. Only three are parrots. Can you tell which one is *not* a parrot?

Red-crowned parakeet

Blue-rumped parrotlet

Blue and yellow macaw

Keel-billed toucan

Traits of Parrots

If you guessed the toucan, you were right. The toucan is a snazzy-looking tropical bird, but it is not a parrot. A parrot has a hooked beak, but a toucan does not.

The beaks of most parrots are strong enough to crack the hardest nuts. Using their thick, hooked beaks, they can carve nests in decaying wood or dig holes in hard dirt. Parrots also use their beaks to groom one another and give other birds a tender nibble. Parrots can even grab onto branches with their beaks.

Parrots have unusual feet. Two toes point forward, and two toes point backward. This type of foot can grip like a hand with fingers and thumbs. Many birds have feet with three toes that point forward and one toe that points backward. These feet work well for running, walking, hopping, or catching *prey*. The birds

These hyacinth macaws have thick, hooked beaks.

6

cannot use their feet to hold food as parrots can.

Only parrots can bring food up to their mouths with their feet. Other birds must lower their heads to eat. Some kinds of parrots use their tongue to turn food around so they can crush it with their strong beaks. Other parrots use their tongues like brushes to lick nectar from flowers.

A parrot's thick tongue and special voice box lets it make many different kinds of sounds. Some parrots can learn to imitate the human voice. They repeat the sounds they hear and often mix them all up together. The result can be a strange hodgepodge of barking dogs, car alarms, whistles, and radio tunes. Suddenly, the "talking" bird will let out a piercing scream and begin all over again. In most cases, the birds don't know what they are

A bare-eyed cockatoo uses its foot to eat a piece of fruit.

saying. Scientists have proven that parrots are among the smartest animals, though.

Most parrots feed their young by *regurgitating* food. The parents store food in the stomach or the *crop*—a special pouch in a bird's throat. When an adult returns to the nest, it throws up the food for the hungry babies.

The Order of Living Things

A tiger has more in common with a house cat than with a daisy. A true bug is more like a butterfly than a jellyfish. Scientists arrange living things into groups based on how they look and how they act. A tiger and a house cat belong to the same group, but a daisy belongs to a different group.

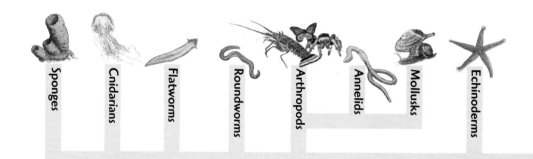

Sponges | Cnidarians | Flatworms | Roundworms | Arthropods | Annelids | Mollusks | Echinoderms

Animals

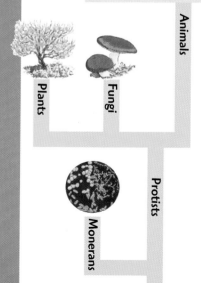

Plants | Fungi

Protists

Monerans

All living things can be placed in one of five groups called *kingdoms*: the plant kingdom, the animal kingdom, the fungus kingdom, the moneran kingdom, or the protist kingdom. You can probably name many of the creatures in the plant and animal kingdoms. The fungus kingdom includes mushrooms, yeasts, and molds. The moneran and protist kingdoms contain thousands of living things that are too small to see without a microscope.

8

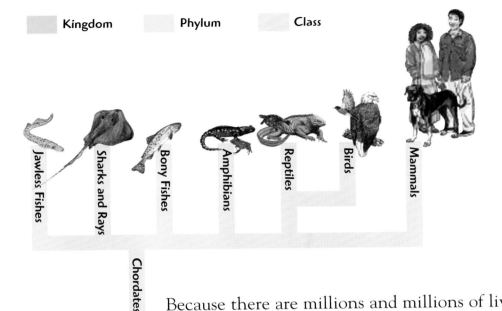

Kingdom **Phylum** **Class**

Jawless Fishes

Sharks and Rays

Bony Fishes

Amphibians

Reptiles

Birds

Mammals

Chordates

Because there are millions and millions of living things on Earth, some of the members of one kingdom may not seem all that similar. The animal kingdom includes creatures as different as tarantulas and trout, jellyfish and jaguars, salamanders and sparrows, elephants and earthworms.

To show that an elephant is more like a jaguar than an earthworm, scientists further separate the creatures in each kingdom into more specific groups. The animal kingdom can be divided into nine *phyla*. Humans belong to the chordate phylum. Almost all chordates have a backbone.

Each phylum can be subdivided into many *classes*. Humans, mice, and elephants all belong to the mammal class. Each class can be further divided into orders; orders into *families*, families into *genera*, and genera into *species*. All the members of a species are very similar.

How Parrots Fit In

You can probably guess that parrots belong to the animal kingdom. They have much more in common with spiders and snakes than with maple trees and morning glories.

Parrots belong to the chordate phylum. Almost all chordates have a backbone and a skeleton. Can you think of other chordates? Examples include elephants, mice, snakes, frogs, fish, and whales.

All birds belong to the same class. There are about thirty orders of birds. Parrot is the common name for the order of birds named *psittaciformes* (SIT-a-see-FOR-meez.) Parrots aren't the only birds in this order, though. Macaws, parakeets, cockatoos, lorikeets, and lovebirds also belong to this group.

Scientists divide parrots into a number of different families and genera. There are more than 300 species of parrots. They can be as small as 3 1/2 inches (9 cm) or as large as 40 inches (102 cm). The feathers of most parrots come in brilliant colors—blues, reds, greens, and yellows. Even the plainest birds usually have some color on their bodies. Parrots live in many different *habitats*—mountains, dry forests, and rain forests—and have many different ways of surviving. In this book, you will learn more about fifteen species of parrots.

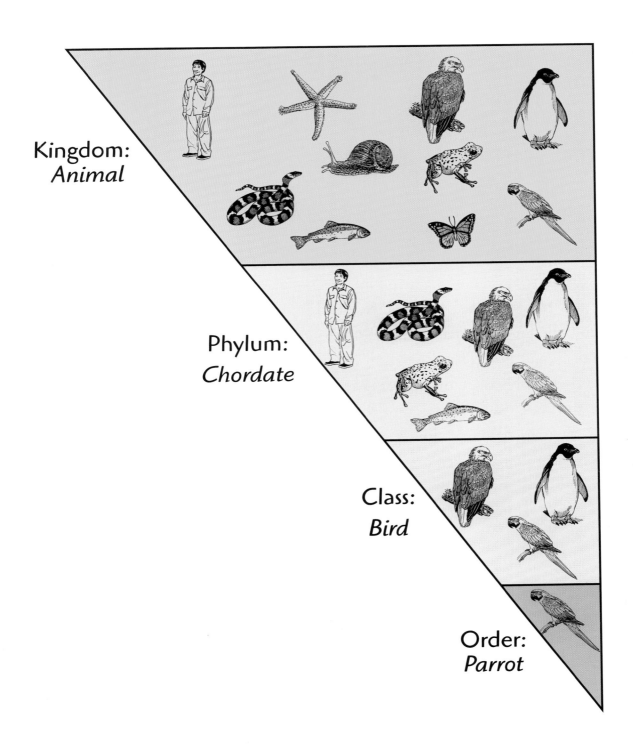

Kingdom: *Animal*

Phylum: *Chordate*

Class: *Bird*

Order: *Parrot*

11

Parakeets

FAMILY: Psittacidae
COMMON EXAMPLE: Budgerigar
GENUS AND SPECIES: *Melopsittacus undulatus*
SIZE: 7 inches (18 cm)

The best-known member of the parrot order is a bird commonly called the parakeet. Many people keep parakeets as pets, but few know the parakeet's real name. This bird comes from Australia, and it's called a budgerigar (BUH-juh-ree-gar) or "budgie" for short. Budgerigar means "good eating" in the language of the *Aborigines*, the native people of Australia. Hawks and lizards eat budgies, and people sometimes eat them too.

Budgerigars are the most plentiful species of parrot. The budgie is a flocking bird. A flock usually has between twenty and several hundred birds. Every so often, though, people in Australia see flocks with as many as 25,000 birds. Huge flocks containing millions of birds fly around the dry woods of Australia.

Most budgies live only 3 or 4 years in the wild, but a pet budgie can live up to 21 years. During its long lifetime, people can train a caged bird to mimic human speech. Most trained parrots can imitate fewer than twenty words. One very talkative budgie, a bird named Sparkie Williams, could mimic more than 530 words.

Cockatoos

FAMILY: Cacatuidae
COMMON EXAMPLE: Black palm cockatoo
GENUS AND SPECIES: *Probosciger aterrimus*
SIZE: 22 to 24 inches (56 to 61 cm)

The black palm cockatoo is one of the three largest species of cockatoos. This bird's scientific name means "long, gloomy, black face." The bird's *crest* of feathers seems to make its face even longer. When it is trying to attract a mate or warn an enemy to stay away, the feathers on its head stand upright and look like a fancy hat.

These gray-black birds have red, naked patches on their faces. The color changes from bright red to pale pink, depending on the bird's health and how excited or upset it is.

Palm cockatoos like to perch in tall trees, where they can watch out for danger. They spend time alone, in pairs, or in small groups. When cockatoos get together, usually early in the morning, they seem to prefer certain meeting spots. No one knows why they like one place better than another.

Palm cockatoos do a few things that almost no other birds do. On rainy mornings, they like to hang upside down with their wings and tails stretched out. Scientists call this the rain-bathing display. Scientists have also seen male cockatoos beat on a hollow trunk with sticks, stones, and nuts. Sometimes the birds drum on a tree as many as 200 times in a row.

Cockatoos

FAMILY: Cacatuidae
COMMON EXAMPLE: Sulfur-crested cockatoo
GENUS AND SPECIES: *Cacatua galerita*
SIZE: 20 inches (51 cm)

Cockatoos are mainly white or black, but the colors under their crests can be shocking pink or yellow. Sulfur-crested cockatoos are not afraid to show their feelings. An excited bird raises its crest, flashes its yellow feathers, and bobs and sways its head in figure eights. When a male wants to get a female's attention, he simply walks out on a branch and hangs upside down, chattering softly. He does not squawk or squeak, but chatters softly for a change.

Cockatoos mate for life. During mating season, they *preen*, or comb, each other's crest feathers and touch bills. The female usually lays two round eggs in a hole in an old tree. A month later, the chicks hatch. They are blind and have no feathers. The parents regurgitate food from their crops for the hungry chicks.

When the young leave the nest, they flock together in large groups. People can see them only from a distance, though. These birds have an "early warning system." A lookout bird stays alert. When a person or a *predator* approaches the flock, the lookout squawks and all the birds take off. They fly away, beating their large wings rapidly and calling loudly.

Lorikeets

FAMILY: Loriidae
COMMON EXAMPLE: Rainbow lorikeet
GENUS AND SPECIES: *Trichoglossus haematodus*
SIZE: 11 inches (28 cm)

Lorikeets and parakeets have similar shapes, but lorikeets are a little larger. A lorikeet has narrow wings, a pointed tail, and an orange beak. Because its beak is too weak to crack open seeds, the bird depends on its tongue. Tiny hairs on the tip of its tongue sop up sweet nectar from flowers.

About fifty species of lorikeets live in Australia and on other Pacific islands. These beautifully colored birds are noisy and active. They tend to gather in small flocks. When rainbow lorikeets find plenty of food, as many as 10,000 birds will flock together.

You might think hiding from enemies would be difficult for such colorful birds, but their feathers blend in with the green leaves and red flowers of tropical trees. The birds bathe by fluttering among those trees after a rainstorm. As they move from tree to tree, they knock water off the leaves.

People in Australia often see rainbow lorikeets in flower gardens. Lorikeets chatter loudly as they fly around the flowering trees in search of a good feeding spot. When they settle down to eat, the birds become quiet. This is a good time for scientists who study lorikeets to get close to the birds.

18

Parrots

FAMILY: Psittacidae
COMMON EXAMPLE: Kakapo
GENUS AND SPECIES: *Strigops habroptilus*
SIZE: 25 inches (64 cm)

The moss-green kakapo is the world's rarest and most unusual parrot. It is found only in New Zealand, a country southeast of Australia. The kakapo lives in holes or burrows underground and comes out only at night. Because it has soft feathers and a rounded, disklike face, people first thought the kakapo was a kind of owl. Its scientific name means "owl-like." There is one important difference between owls and kakapos, however. Owls eat meat, but kakapos feed on grasses and herbs.

The kakapo is the heaviest parrot in the world. A male can weigh up to 8 pounds (3.5 kg). This parrot has very short wings, and it is too heavy to fly, but it can climb trees. A kakapo can also glide downhill from a tree. This bird usually lives alone and spends most of its time on the ground.

When it is time to mate, males call to females by beating their stubby wings against their big chests. Scientists call this behavior "booming." The males boom up to 7 hours a night for 3 or 4 months! Females mate with the

males that make the loudest boom. A female lays 2 or 3 eggs every 2 to 4 years. Kakapos mate only when they know they can find plenty of food for their chicks.

People and predators hunted kakapos until they were almost all gone. To save these birds, the New Zealand Wildlife Service recently moved them to islands where scientists can protect them. No one knows whether the kakapo will survive.

Parrots

FAMILY: Psittacidae
COMMON EXAMPLE: Kea
GENUS AND SPECIES: *Nestor notabilis*
SIZE: 18 inches (46 cm)

Most parrots live in warm areas, but keas live in the mountains of New Zealand. During winter storms, the birds huddle in burrows protected from rain and snow. On sunny days, they bask in the warmth on rock ledges or roll around in the snow.

Keas are mostly olive-green in color, but they have bright red underwings and dark red rump and tail feathers. You can see a kea's colors only when it flies. In the strong mountain winds, these playful birds often glide in large circles, crying, "kee-aah! kee-aah! kee-aah!"

Keas nest among rocks, under tree roots, or in dead trees. The female lays 2 or 3 eggs and sits on them for 24 days. The male guards the nest from a lookout point.

Keas feed on roots, buds, berries, and flowers. The also eat insects, and sometimes even take a nip out of a dead sheep. In the past, shepherds thought keas killed sheep, so New Zealand hunters killed many of the birds. When people realized that keas don't kill sheep, they began to protect the birds.

Keas do not fear humans. They scavenge for food near ski lodges and hiking shelters. These birds are curious about everything—they will even nibble on rubber windshield-wiper blades and car tires.

Macaws

FAMILY: Psittacidae
COMMON EXAMPLE: Blue and yellow macaw
GENUS AND SPECIES: *Ara ararauna*
SIZE: 33 inches (84 cm)

Blue and yellow macaws are the most common kind of macaws in Central and South America. That may be partly because these birds can survive in so many different habitats. They live in rain forests, open woodlands, marshlands, and grassy areas.

In the wild, blue and yellow macaws live between 30 to 45 years. They spend time in pairs, family groups, or small flocks. Macaws mate for life, and they are always together, watching out for each other. These birds avoid enemies by sitting very still in the tops of trees. You could walk underneath a macaw without even knowing it was there.

Macaws don't make good pets. They scream loudly, and they have the strongest bite in the bird world. A macaw can crack tough Brazil nuts with its powerful beak. These birds also eat fruits, flowers, leaves, and seeds, but you probably wouldn't like their food. Most of the plants have chemicals that taste bad. The bad taste warns animals that the plant has poisons that will make them sick.

So how can blue and yellow macaws eat these poisonous plants? After a meal, they fly to a riverbank and eat clay. Scientists think the clay keeps the poisons in the plants from harming the birds.

Parrots

FAMILY: Psittacidae
COMMON EXAMPLE: Yellow-headed Amazon
GENUS AND SPECIES: *Amazona ochrocephala*
SIZE: 14 inches (36 cm)

Yellow-headed Amazons spend a lot of time grooming their beautiful feathers. They preen themselves and one another with their tongues and beaks. Like many other kinds of parrots, they have special feathers called powder down. The powder down feathers crumble into a dust that the parrots rub into their feathers to help remove body oil and dirt. Yellow-headed Amazons also like to bathe in rivers near their forest homes.

These colorful birds are very hard to see high in the treetops, but you can't avoid hearing them. Parrots are the noisiest birds in the forest. They stay in constant communication with one another, which helps keep flocks together.

Yellow-headed Amazons build their nests in tall, dead trees. When they move around in trees, they don't fly. They climb from branch to branch instead. The female sits on the nest, and the male brings her food. She gets out of the nest to eat. When she's eaten enough for the day, the male joins the other parrots, leaving her alone with her eggs.

Parrotlets

FAMILY: Psittacidae
COMMON EXAMPLE: Green-rumped parrotlet
GENUS AND SPECIES: *Forpus passerinus*
SIZE: 5 inches (13 cm)

Parrotlets are tiny parakeets with short tails. They are among the smallest parrots in the world. Flocks of parrotlets whiz along, flying in a zigzag pattern to avoid hawks. The birds dip down, then swoop up to land in a tree. They may decide to eat some grass seeds in a cattle pasture before flitting off to another tree to eat berries. Parrotlets live along the edges of fields and in parks and gardens.

The males have a bluish tinge to their wings, but otherwise their feathers are bright green. These colors help them hide from enemies. Since they are about the same size and the same color as a leaf, they are almost impossible to see in the treetops. When these birds feed in large numbers and chatter "chee, chee, chee," it can seem as if the trees are talking.

During the nesting season, a pair of parrotlets might take over an abandoned bird's nest in a fence post or enlarge a hole that was hollowed out by woodpeckers. The female lays between three and seven white eggs on wood chips in her snug nest.

Green-rumped parrotlets are found around villages in Guyana, Suriname, and French Guiana, countries that border the Atlantic Ocean at the top of South America.

Parakeets

FAMILY: Psittacidae
EXAMPLE: Carolina parakeet
GENUS AND SPECIES: *Conuropis carolinensis*
SIZE: 12 inches (30 cm)

Carolina parakeets were once common throughout the southeastern United States. Unfortunately, they are now *extinct*. These birds disappeared for several reasons. The parakeets lost their habitat when early settlers cut down the forests to make room for farms and orchards. Then people shot the parakeets when the birds raided their fruit trees. Whenever a Carolina parakeet was shot, other birds in the flock would fly around the fallen bird. This made it easy for farmers to kill many more parakeets.

These parakeets slept in hollow trees. Their hooked beaks helped them hold on to tree trunks while they dozed. About an hour after sunrise, the screeching flock would fly through the woods to a nearby creek and take a long drink. When the orange, yellow, and green birds landed, they covered the ground like a colorful carpet.

By 1831, the famous bird artist John James Audubon was worried that Carolina parakeets would not survive. He was right.

When people realized that the parakeets were becoming rare, they tried to breed them in zoos. The last bird died in the Cincinnati Zoo in 1918. Some scientists think a few wild birds might have lasted until 1938 in the swamps of South Carolina, but now they are all gone.

Parrots

FAMILY: Psittacidae

EXAMPLE: Thick-billed parrot

GENUS AND SPECIES: *Rhynchopsitta pachyrhyncha*

SIZE: 15 inches (38 cm)

Many years ago, flocks of thick-billed parrots migrated north from Mexico into Arizona each year. The birds were common and very tame. Eventually, the thick-billed parrots stopped coming, though. People had cut down the pine forests the birds needed for food and shelter. Today these birds are in danger of disappearing from Earth forever. A few thick-billed parrots still survive in the mountains of Mexico, but they too may soon be gone.

These emerald-green parrots have bright red shoulder patches. They use their thick beaks to slice open pinecones so that they can eat the seeds. They also crack open acorns. In the winter, thick-billed parrots sometimes get the water they need by biting icicles off a frozen waterfall or scooping up beakfuls of snow.

Like most parrots, these birds are strong fliers. They soar on updrafts of air like gliders. If a predator, such as a red-tailed hawk, gets too close, a whole flock of thick-billed parrots will fly up and whirl around the enemy to drive it away.

In the early 1990s, biologists tried to reintroduce twenty-nine thick-billed parrots to Arizona. When scientists released the parrots,

the birds had trouble finding food and avoiding predators. The flock had no older, more experienced parrots to lead the way. Eventually, all the birds died.

Parakeets

FAMILY: Psittacidae
COMMON EXAMPLE: Monk parakeet
GENUS AND SPECIES: *Myiopsitta monachus*
SIZE: 12 inches (30 cm)

Monk parakeets are originally from South America, but these birds have made homes as far north as Chicago, Illinois. During the late 1960s, pet stores imported thousands of monk parakeets. Some of them escaped from their owners' homes. Then several cages of these birds broke open at Kennedy Airport in New York City, and more birds escaped. The parakeets found food at feeders in backyards and were able to adapt to their new habitats.

At first, people thought that monk parakeets would become pests and eat farmers' crops. Fortunately, the number of birds in a given area has never grown large enough to cause much damage.

Like all parakeets, monk parakeets have long, pointed tails and wings. They live together in nests that are like noisy apartment houses. Monk parakeets are the only parrots that build stick nests. One giant nest may be up to 9 feet (3 m) high, weigh more than 100 pounds (45 kg), and have as many as twenty compartments.

During the summer, chicks crowd the nests. In the cold winter, entire families huddle into the nests to stay warm. Each chamber has a bottom entrance so that predators cannot get inside.

Parrots

FAMILY: Psittacidae
COMMON EXAMPLE: African gray parrot
GENUS AND SPECIES: *Psittacus erithacus*
SIZE: 13 inches (33 cm)

The large continent of Africa has only a dozen species of parrots. The best known—and smartest—is the African gray parrot. Roman leaders, such as Julius Caesar, kept African grays as pets. One ruler fed the parrots' bodies to the lions and ate the brains himself!

Scientists have recently discovered what the Roman leaders knew—parrots are very smart birds. They may be among the most intelligent animals in the world. Experiments with an African gray parrot named Alex showed that he can identify 80 objects using more than 100 words and symbols.

These beautiful but shy parrots live in central Africa. They can live in forests, woodlands, and areas near the sea, but they avoid places where humans live. During the day, they travel in pairs or small groups. At dusk, they gather in large flocks and roost in tree-tops. These birds make quite a racket.

In the early morning, the flock scatters into the surrounding forests to feed. Sometimes, the birds fly down to the ground to eat small rocks. Grit helps them digest the seeds, nuts, and berries they find in the treetops of the tropical forests. The only other time these birds leave the trees is to drink from a river or lake.

Lovebirds

FAMILY: Psittacidae
COMMON EXAMPLE: Fischer's lovebird
GENUS AND SPECIES: *Agapornis fischeri*
SIZE: 6 inches (15 cm)

Few birds are more social than lovebirds. They show great affection for each other. Nibbling each other around the head is part of the bonding behavior between mates. Scientists call this behavior *mutual preening*. A bird can't scratch its own neck or head, so its mate does the job.

Like many other parrots, Fischer's lovebirds mate for life. These birds take togetherness even further than most parrots. They seem to want to be together all the time. They appear to need body contact with each other. When the birds are apart, they seem stressed. When they are reunited, they seem happy. Their affectionate behavior makes them desirable pets. Lovebirds have been popular cage birds since Englishwomen kept the first ones in the late 1500s.

Fischer's lovebirds live in thornbushes, grasslands, and farmlands in central Africa. Flocks of twenty to eighty to several hundred birds often gather to feed. Much of the time, they feed noisily on the ground in the dry woodlands. They are not shy, but if an intruder gets too close, the birds suddenly become very quiet. Then they fly off, twittering and whistling.

Parrots

FAMILY: Psittacidae
COMMON EXAMPLE: Rose-ringed parakeet
GENUS AND SPECIES: *Psittacula krameri*
SIZE: 14 to 16 inches (36 to 41 cm)

Rose-ringed parakeets are originally from Africa and Asia, but today they also live in California, Florida, Hawaii, Venezuela, Great Britain, Holland, Belgium, Egypt, and Israel. Early explorers captured the birds and brought them to these new places. Wherever rose-ringed parakeets go, they thrive.

These long-tailed parrots are mostly green and yellow-green. They get their name from the pink collar or "rose ring" around their neck. The male has a black throat, but the female does not.

Rose-ringed parakeets are very common in India, where they nest under tile roofs. Large flocks of these birds—sometimes as many as 1,000 of them—often invade fields and orchards. Even scarecrows posted on platforms around the fields don't keep out the hungry parakeets. When the farmers arrive to chase the parakeets away, the lookout bird screeches a loud warning. The whole flock bursts into flight, and the parakeets quickly disappear.

During the mating season, rose-ringed parakeets make soft, twittering sounds. The female moves her head in a half-circle, opens the pupils of her eyes wide, and spreads her wings. The male gives her food, and then the birds mate. They take turns sitting on the eggs.

Parrots in Danger

Today, parrots are in danger throughout the world. Fourteen kinds of parrots have disappeared from Earth forever, and another ninety species may soon vanish too. One parrot species, the Spix macaw, is down to just a couple of wild birds. In the 1980s, trappers caught every Spix macaw they could find and brought them to zoos and other safe places. More than forty of these birds now live in captivity. Scientists hope that these birds may be able to survive and have plenty of chicks.

Spix macaw

Most parrot species are in danger because people have destroyed their natural habitats. Humans have cut down tropical rain forests for firewood and to make room for ranches. The pine-forest homes of other parrots were cut down for lumber. Other species are sold as pets. Until recently, most of the parrots that people bought and sold were caught in the wild. Several hundred years of making pets out of wild parrots has taken its toll.

Some types of parrots are so valuable that people cut down trees with nests to get at the chicks. The adult birds then have nowhere to nest, so they leave the habitat. Collectors sometimes smuggle the young birds out of the forests. They hide them in suitcases and send them to cities in other parts of the world. Most chicks die during the trip. The birds that live can be sold for thousands of dollars.

An international law that recently banned the buying and selling of all wild birds is starting to have an effect. Most of the birds sold in pet shops are now raised in captivity, but some rare birds are still smuggled into the United States. Several nations show rare and endangered parrots on their postage stamps to increase public awareness.

Protecting parrots and their habitats has helped some birds. In 1975, only thirteen Puerto Rican parrots were left in the wild. Protection and education helped save these birds.

Puerto Rican parrot

Many people want to help save parrots, parakeets, cockatoos, macaws, lorikeets, and lovebirds. Their beauty and their ability to act and "talk" like humans make them some of the most interesting animals in the world. We don't want to lose any more of these bold and beautiful parrots if we can help it.

Words to Know

Aborigines—the native people of Australia

class—a group of creatures within a phylum that share certain characteristics

crest—feathers that stand up on top of a bird's head

crop—a special pouch or sac in a bird's throat

extinct—a species that has died out

family—a group of creatures within an order that share certain characteristics

genus (plural **genera**)—a group of creatures within a family that share certain characteristics

habitat—the environment where a species lives and grows

kingdom—one of the five divisions into which all living things are placed: the animal kingdom, the plant kingdom, the fungus kingdom, the moneran kingdom, and the protist kingdom

mutual preening—a behavior in which a pair of birds comb each other's feathers

order—a group of creatures within a class that share certain characteristics

phylum (plural **phyla**)—a group of creatures within a kingdom that share certain characteristics

predator—an animal that hunts other animals for food

preen—to comb and straighten out feathers

prey—an animal that is hunted and eaten by another animal

Psittaciformes (SIT-a-see-FOR-meez)—the order of birds that includes parrots, parakeets, lorikeets, lovebirds, cockatoos, and macaws

regurgitate—to transfer food to young by bringing it up from the stomach or crop

species—a group of creatures within a genus that share certain characteristics. Members of a species can mate and produce young.

Learning More

Books

Bailey, Jill. *Save the Macaw.* Orlando, FL: Raintree/Steck-Vaughn, 1992.

Gabin, Martin. *Your First Parrot.* Neptune City, NJ: T.F.H. Publications, 1991.

Halaburda, Tammy. *A Basic Book of Lovebirds: Look and Learn.* Neptune City, NJ: T.F.H. Publications, 1994.

Juniper, Tony and Michael Parr. *Parrots: A Guide to Parrots of the World.* New Haven, CT: Yale University Press, 1998.

Rauzon, Mark. *Parrots.* Danbury, CT: Franklin Watts, 1996.

Vrbova, Zusa, et al. *Parakeets.* New York: Chelsea House, 1998.

Web Sites

The Complete Lexicon of Parrots
http://www.parrot-lexicon.com
This site supplies information about habits, habitats, diet, social interaction, and more for dozens of species.

The Fabulous Kakapo
http://www.kakapo.net
This site is dedicated to the flightless kakapo, the world's "rarest and strangest parrot."

Parrot Society of Australia
http://www.parrotsociety.org.au/clubs/links.htm
This site provides links to promote "parrot keeping, breeding, and conservation throughout the world."

Index

About the Author

Mark J. Rauzon is a wildlife biologist and a writer-photographer who travels widely. He has worked as a biologist for the U.S. Fish and Wildlife Service in Alaska and Hawaii. He has also written many children's books about animals, including *Seabirds*, *Hummingbirds*, *Vultures*, and *Golden Eagles of Devil Mountain* for Franklin Watts. Rauzon lives in Oakland, California, with his wife and black cat.